BOOK ONE

A DOZEN A DAY

Technical Exercises
FOR THE PIANO
to be done each day
BEFORE practicing

by

Edna Mae Burnam

Includes Online Audio Orchestrations by Ric Ianonne

PLAYBACK+
Speed • Pitch • Balance • Loop

The exclusive **PLAYBACK+** feature allows tempo changes without altering the pitch.
Loop points can also be set for repetition of tricky measures.

To access audio, visit:
www.halleonard.com/mylibrary

Enter Code
2434-6203-0885-3745

ISBN 978-1-4584-1975-0

WILLIS MUSIC

EXCLUSIVELY DISTRIBUTED BY

HAL•LEONARD®

Visit Hal Leonard Online at
www.halleonard.com

Contact us:
Hal Leonard
7777 West Bluemound Road
Milwaukee, WI 53213
Email: info@halleonard.com

In Europe, contact:
Hal Leonard Europe Limited
42 Wigmore Street
Marylebone, London, W1U 2RN
Email: info@halleonardeurope.com

In Australia, contact:
Hal Leonard Australia Pty. Ltd.
4 Lentara Court
Cheltenham, Victoria, 3192 Australia
Email: info@halleonard.com.au

To my family

PREFACE

Many people do exercises every morning before they go to work.

Likewise, we should give our fingers exercises every day before we begin our practicing.

The purpose of this book is to help develop strong hands and flexible fingers.

Do not try to learn the entire first dozen exercises the first week you study this book! Learn two or three exercises, and do them each day before practicing. When these are mastered, add another, then another, and keep adding until the twelve exercises can be played perfectly.

When the first dozen—or Group I—has been mastered and perfected, Group II may be introduced in the same manner, and so on for the other Groups.

Many of these exercises may be transposed to different keys. In fact, this should be encouraged.

EDNA MAE BURNAM

INDEX

Group I

1. Walking and Running

1

1st time—legato (smooth, connected)
2nd time—staccato (sharp, detached)

2. Skipping

2

legato—staccato

3. Hopping

3

staccato

6

4. Deep Breathing

5. Deep Knee Bend

6. Stretching

7. Stretching Right Leg Up

8. Stretching Left Leg

9. Cartwheels

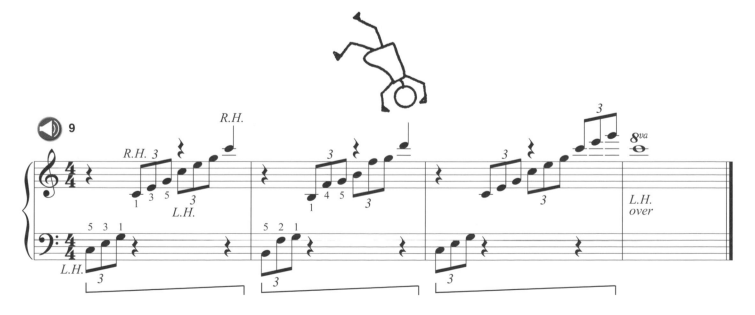

8

10. The Splits

 10

legato—staccato

11. Standing on Head

11

legato—staccato

12. Fit as a Fiddle and Ready To Go

12

legato—staccato

Group II
1. Morning Stretch

4. High Stepping

legato—staccato

16

5. Jumping

17

6. Kicking Right Leg

18

7. Kicking Left Leg

8. The Splits

9. Leg Work (lying down)

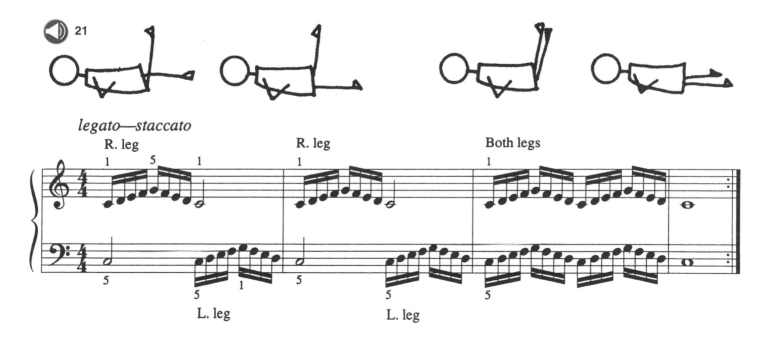

10. Sitting Up and Lying Down

11. A Hard Trick

Now do the whole trick:

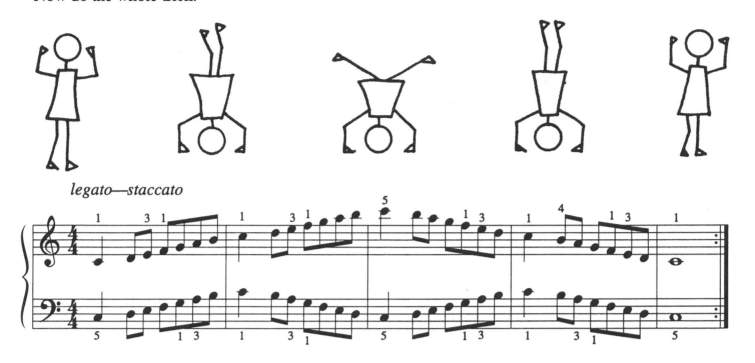

legato—staccato

12. Fit as a Fiddle and Ready To Go

Group III

1. Deep Breathing

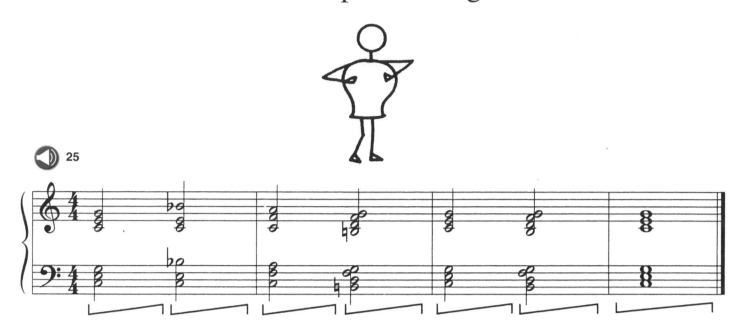

2. Rolling

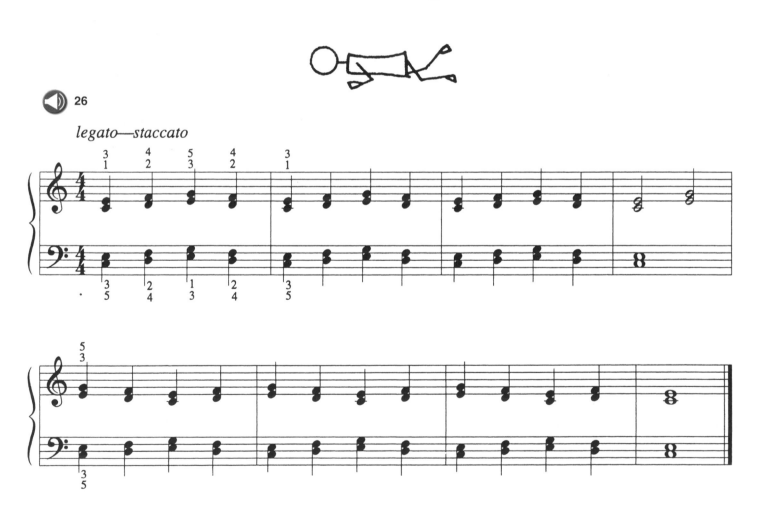

3. Climbing (in place)

27

legato—staccato

4. Tiptoe Running (in place)

28

16

5. Baby Steps

legato—staccato

29

6. Giant Steps

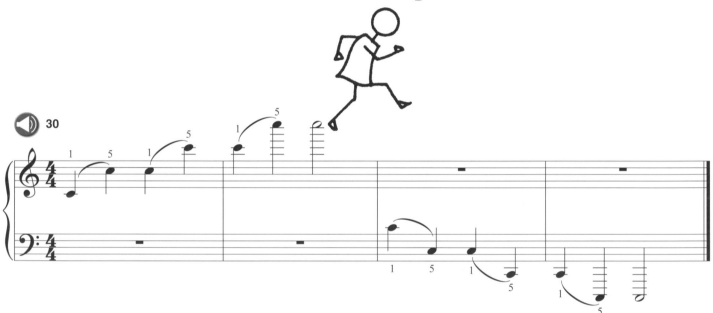

30

7. Jumping Rope

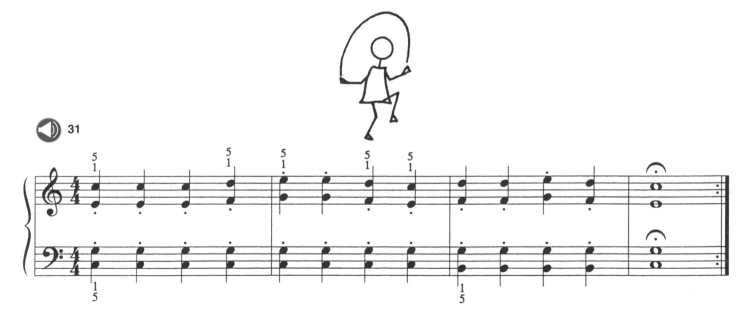

31

8. Somersaults

9. Touching Toes

10. Ballet Exercise ("Entre chat quatre")

11. The Splits

🔊 35

legato—staccato

12. Fit as a Fiddle and Ready To Go

🔊 36

legato—staccato

Group IV

1. Morning Stretch

2. Climbing (in place)

3. Tiptoe Running (in place)

4. Running

5. Cartwheels

6. Touching Toes

7. Hopping

8. Baby Steps

9. Giant Steps

10. Flinging Arms Out and Back

legato—staccato

11. Standing on Head

12. Fit as a Fiddle and Ready To Go

Group V
1. Deep Breathing

49

2. Touching Toes

50

3. Hopping

4. Climbing a Ladder

legato—staccato

5. Jumping Rope (Slow, and "Red Pepper")

🔊 53

Slow

"Red Pepper"

6. Swinging Arms

🔊 54

legato—staccato

7. Hand Springs

8. Walking Like a Duck

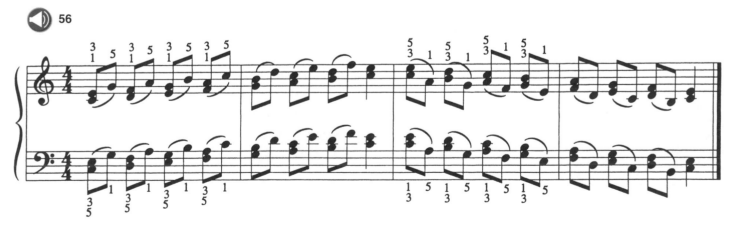

9. Bear Walk

57

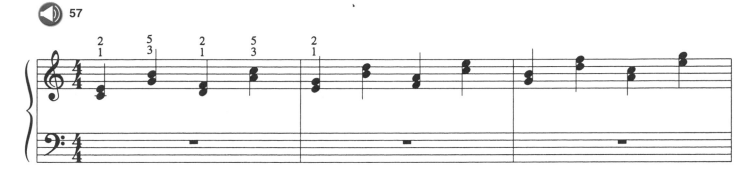

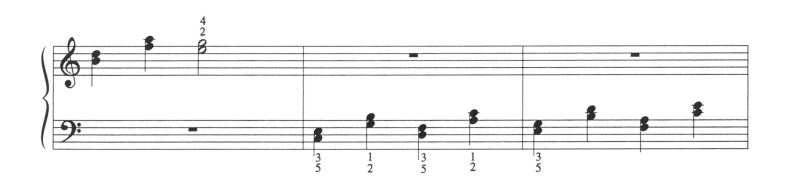

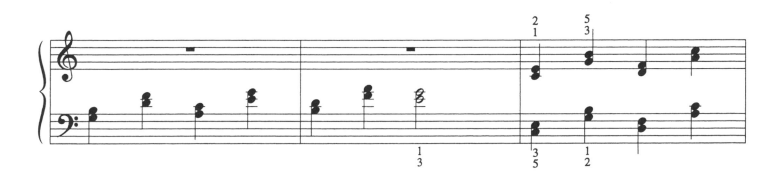

10. Sliding Down the Bannister

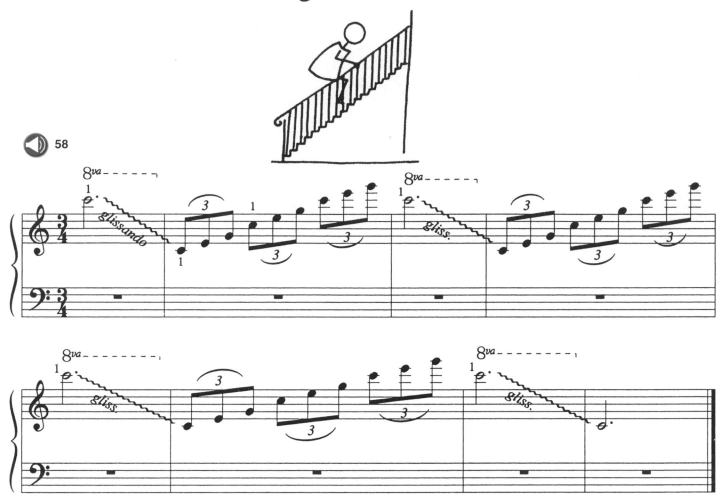

11. A Hard Trick

Practice this first:

legato—staccato

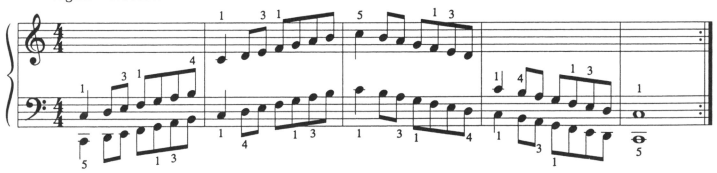

Now practice this:

legato—staccato

Now do the whole trick:

legato—staccato

12. Fit as a Fiddle and Ready To Go